W9-BCN-828

READY TO MAKE
MUSIC

# IS THE
# FLUTE
# FOR YOU?

ELAINE LANDAU

Lerner Publications Company · Minneapolis

Copyright © 2011 by Lerner Publishing Group, Inc.

Lerner Publications Company
A division of Lerner Publishing Group, Inc.
241 First Avenue North
Minneapolis, MN 55401 U.S.A.

Website address: www.lernerbooks.com


Library of Congress Cataloguing-in-Publication Data

Landau, Elaine.
    Is the flute for you? / by Elaine Landau.
        p.   cm. — (Ready to make music)
    Includes bibliographical references and index.
    ISBN 978-0-7613-5420-8 (lib. bdg. : alk. paper)
    1. Flute—Juvenile literature  I. Title.
ML935.L36  2011
788.3′219—dc22              2744                    2009048970

Manufactured in the United States of America
1 – DP – 7/15/10

# CONTENTS

# CHAPTER ONE

# THE FABULOUS FLUTE

## Picture this:

You're a flutist in a symphony orchestra. Tonight's the night you've waited for. You're playing an important solo. You've practiced for weeks for this moment, and you play wonderfully. The sound coming out of your flute is flawless. The conductor and audience are all smiles. Everyone loves beautiful music. That's what you've created tonight, and you couldn't be prouder.

Practice time pays off when you have an important flute solo at a concert.

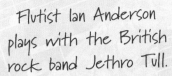
Flutist Ian Anderson plays with the British rock band Jethro Tull.

Switch to this scene. You're a flutist with a popular rock group. Your fabulous flute melodies make your band stand out. You're known as rock's Pied Piper. Your band is playing to a packed house tonight. Soon it's time for your solo. The notes seem to dance out of your instrument. The audience loves you. They go wild for the sound of your flute.

Wait a minute. Something's wrong. A flute in a rock group?

No. You read it right. The flute's a versatile instrument. Rock and classical artists alike have praised its clear, sweet sound.

Can you see yourself playing the flute? That just might be a great choice for you. There are lots of good reasons to pick the flute. Here are just a few.

## EASY TO CARRY

The flute is fairly small and light. You don't have to be an Olympic weight lifter to carry one to school. You'll also find the

## WE ARE FAMILY

People live in families. You're part of a family. Family members often have some things in common. Do you have your dad's eyes? Your mom's laugh? Or maybe most of the people in your family wear glasses—including you.

Flutes and other woodwind instruments are often part of school orchestra groups.

Instruments are grouped in families too. The flute is a member of the woodwind family. So what do woodwind instruments have in common? All of them are played by blowing air either over or through them. Musicians use vibrating or moving air to create all sorts of different sounds on woodwind instruments.

The piccolo has the highest pitch of any woodwind instrument. A piccolo is a small, shrill type of flute. An instrument called the bassoon has the lowest pitch. Woodwind instruments such as the oboe, the clarinet, and the saxophone fall somewhere in between.

flute is easy to take apart and put back together. It fits nicely in a locker. The same can't be said for a piano or a tuba.

## NOT SO HARD TO CARE FOR

The flute doesn't need a lot of daily upkeep. Students just have to make sure their flutes stay clean and dry. Even younger players can learn to give these instruments the tender loving care they deserve.

## THE PRICE IS RIGHT

Some instruments are extremely costly. Even a used piano can cost more than many families can afford. This isn't the case with the flute. You can get a student model for around $350. Families looking to spend less can buy or rent a used flute. This can save a lot of money. A flute doesn't have to be new or shiny to sound great. Much of the sound depends on how good the player is.

## WOW! WHAT AN INSTRUMENT

Of course, the best reason to play the flute is because you love its sound and really want to play it. Flutist Kat Epple put it this way: "You need to love playing the flute. When you are picking an instrument, pick the one you love. Don't choose the one someone else thinks you should play. When you start to play the flute, it may take a while to get your first really clear note. But when you finally do, it's worth it."

# PARTS OF THE FLUTE

Your body is made up of many different parts. You've got a head, a trunk, arms, legs, and other parts. Take a look at a flute. It might seem like a 2-foot (0.6-meter)-long tube. But like you, the flute is made up of several parts. Let's take a closer look at them.

## KEYS

Flutists use the keys to play different notes. Pressing down on the keys and letting go opens and closes the flute's tone holes (small openings drilled into the flute). This lets the flute make a range of sounds. Each key has a key pad beneath it. The keys also have small springs. The springs are connected to the keys. They allow the keys to move up and down.

## FOOT JOINT

The foot joint has some keys and tone holes. Flutists use their pinkie fingers to play the keys on the foot joint.

## HEAD JOINT

The head joint is the part of the flute that's held closest to your mouth. You won't find any keys on the head joint. But you will find the lip plate and the mouth hole.

## LIP PLATE

The lip plate—also known as the embouchure plate—is where your lower lip rests when you play the flute.

## MOUTH HOLE

The mouth hole is a small opening on the lip plate. A flute player blows air over the mouth hole to produce a sound.

## BODY JOINT

The body joint is the longest part of the flute. Both the head joint and the foot joint connect to it. Most of the flute's keys are on the body joint.

# CHAPTER TWO

# SO MANY WAYS TO PLAY

Just what types of music can the flute be used to play? See if you can pick the correct answer—or answers—below.

A. classical

B. jazz and blues

C. rock

D. country

E. folk and world music

F. all of the above and more

Was your answer F? If so, you got it right! Flutists are creative. They've found lots of ways to make great music with their instrument.

Flutists play many types of music, such as classical, jazz, and rock.

# ROCKIN' WITH THE FLUTE

Does the idea of a flutist in a rock band still seem strange to you? Well, lots of rock groups that came to fame in the 1960s feature the flute. The Moody Blues is one of them.

The Moody Blues hit the music scene back in 1967. This British band came up with their own blend of rock and classical music. The flute is central to their distinctive sound. The Moody Blues' arty brand of rock has won them an army of devoted fans. It has also won them more than a few music awards. Over the years, other groups have copied their style.

Jethro Tull is another group famous for its use of the flute. This band formed around the same time as the Moody Blues. Jethro Tull's music mixes rock, blues, and folk. Jethro Tull's lead singer, Ian Anderson, is a highly accomplished flute player. He uses the flute as his main instrument. He was among the first leads in a rock band to do so.

Ray Thomas performs on the flute with the Moody Blues.

Are you an aspiring flutist who'd like to be part of the rock scene? Then listen to rock music that features the flute. The more you listen, the more you'll learn about how the flute can be used in rock.

# SPOTLIGHT ON THE MARSHALL TUCKER BAND

Is it country, or is it rock? That's a question lots of people ask when they hear the Marshall Tucker Band. Formed in Spartanburg, South Carolina, in 1972, the band has been described as a bunch of good ol' boys. They blend country, rock, and gospel to make a sound that's all their own.

What makes the Marshall Tucker Band so special? It's partly their use of the flute. The lilting sound of the instrument has made many of the band's recordings stand out.

The group's appeal can't be denied. The Marshall Tucker Band has sold millions of records. It's also had hit singles and sold out many concerts.

David Muse plays flute with the Marshall Tucker Band at a concert in 2007.

**Herbie Mann is a well-known jazz flutist.**

# A JAZZY INSTRUMENT

Are you more into jazz than rock? Then you're in luck, because there's definitely a place for flutists in the jazz world. As early as 1956, the well-known jazz publication *DownBeat Magazine* was handing out Best Flutist Awards for jazz.

Herbie Mann is often regarded as the first modern jazz flutist. While several other jazz musicians have also played the flute, Mann was one of the first to base his career on it. He did some of his best work in the 1950s and 1960s.

Mann often recorded with Sam Most, another important flutist of that time. Most is credited with coming up with new ways to use the flute. He developed the technique of humming into the flute while playing it. Quite a few jazz flutists later used this technique.

Jazz flute music is not highly structured. Jazz musicians often make up parts of their music as they play it. This is known as improvisation. It lets jazz musicians develop their own style musically. Improvisation also sets jazz apart from most other playing styles.

Do you dream of becoming a great jazz flutist? Start preparing for it now. Listen to recordings by flutists who play jazz. Get a feel for how their music sounds. After a while, you can try to play along with them.

## THE CLASSICAL FLUTE

Of course, the flute is still most often used in classical music. Did you first fall in love with the sound of the classical flute? Many flutists, such as Sir James Galway and Jean-Pierre Rampal, have.

Sir James Galway performs in 2005.

# MEET THE CLARINET

The flute can be used to play an incredible variety of music. But what if you're not sure it's for you? Then maybe you'll want to try the clarinet, a woodwind cousin of the flute.

The clarinet is a popular instrument for band students. Like the flute, it's fairly small and light. You'll have no trouble carrying it around with you. The clarinet also has a very beautiful sound. Its tone is rich and velvety.

Do you think you'd play the clarinet the same way you play the flute? Well, not quite. Unlike the flute, the clarinet is a reed instrument. Reed instruments have reeds (thin pieces of wood, metal, or plastic) in their mouthpieces. Players blow air over the reeds to produce a sound. Some reed instruments—like the clarinet— have single reeds. Others— like the bassoon, the English horn, and the oboe—have double reeds.

The clarinet is a popular instrument for school band students.

Some of the world's greatest classical composers have written music for the flute. Two of these are Wolfgang Amadeus Mozart and Ludwig van Beethoven. Galway and Rampal have made brilliant careers out of playing music by these and many other composers.

Galway and Rampal took on solo careers. But most classical flutists play in orchestras or symphonic bands. Other classical flutists play in smaller musical groups. These are known as ensembles.

Practice is important for flutists no matter what kinds of music they play.

# A LITTLE BIT OF FLUTE HISTORY

The flute has been used to play classical music for many centuries. Starting around the mid-1700s, musicians in Europe used wooden flutes to play this style of music. In the 1830s, a classical musician named Theobald Boehm developed a metal flute. Boehm's flute had the same system of keys and tone holes used in modern-day flutes.

Flutists in orchestras began playing Boehm's flute. It gave the flutists more control over their pitch. These days, most flutes used in orchestras are silver (pictured right). These flutes closely resemble the instrument Boehm created more than 150 years ago.

Do you hope to play classical flute someday? Want to be good enough to be noticed? Then learn all you can about classical flute. If you can, try to see some live performances. Maybe when you're older, you'll be onstage with the best of them.

# CHAPTER THREE

# THE FLUTE AND YOU:
## A PERFECT PAIR?

This is an exciting time for you. You've decided to learn to play an instrument, and you're pretty sure you want to try the flute. Is that the right choice? There's no easy answer to this question. Different people choose the flute for different reasons.

Some kids want to play an instrument they're familiar with. Maybe their parents or a brother or sister plays the flute. Perhaps they've always loved the flute music an aunt or a cousin plays. That's how it was for flutist Carol Naveira-Nicholson.

It can be fun to study the flute with someone in your family.

# MEET THE BASSOON

Perhaps you like the flute, but you've always pictured yourself playing a larger musical instrument. Then maybe the bassoon is for you.

The bassoon has a low, deep sound. It may be best described as rich and mellow. The bassoon is also among the largest of woodwind instruments.

The bassoon has two reeds that are tied together and placed inside a tube at the top of the instrument. When you blow air between the reeds, the two pieces of wood vibrate (move back and forth). This vibration creates the full, warm sound for which the bassoon is known.

Have you ever heard the distinctive voice of the bassoon? It's enough to make you fall in love with the instrument.

"My father was a drummer," she explained. "I used to hang out with my dad and his friends. Someone was always asking me what I played. It was just expected that I'd play an instrument. I'd seen my aunt play the flute, so I tried it. It turned out to be right for me."

Sometimes young people pick an instrument when they enter a band program at school. They may not always end up with their first-choice instrument. For example, a student might wind up playing the oboe instead of the flute because of his or her particular mouth shape. Or the instrument a student wants may already be taken. But other times, you just might get lucky.

Flutist Cynthia Kivlan really wanted to play the flute. Yet things didn't look very hopeful for her when she started her school's music program. "I told the band director that I wanted to play the flute," she recalled. "He said that he already had too many flute players and suggested the

Many students pick an instrument to play when they join their school's band program.

Check Out Receipt

Clifton Park-Halfmoon Public Library
518-371-8622
http://www.cphlibrary.org/

Wednesday, September 5, 2018 4:20:33 PM
40318

Item: 0000603732744
Title: Is the flute for you?
Material: Book
Due: 10/03/2018

The value of the materials you borrowed toda
y is $27.93.


Clifton Park-Halfmoon Public Library
Your Community Center for Lifelong Learning.

clarinet. But I had my heart set on the flute. I began to cry and walked out of his class. That evening the band director phoned my mother. He told her that he had an extra flute for me. He said he'd love to have me in the class. So the next day, I was given my own beautiful shiny flute to take home and practice on."

## MEET THE RECORDER

Not sure you're quite ready for the flute? Maybe you should think about playing the recorder. The recorder is closely related to the flute, but it's easier to play.

The recorder is popular in school music programs. Many students play it before choosing a band instrument. It's good practice for learning to play the flute. Don't think of the recorder as a plastic children's toy. It's an instrument with a great history. In early times, it was played in the courts of kings and queens. These days, the recorder is making a comeback. Serious musicians are playing the recorder again in bands.

Still other people just seem to be drawn to a particular instrument. Flutist Christine Soroka knew the flute was for her before she entered elementary school. She described her experience in this way.

When I was three years old, my dad took me to a parade, and I saw the marchers with their flutes. The flutes were so beautiful. I imagined what it would feel

These elementary school students play in a band with flutes, guitars, and violins.

Flute and piccolo players often play in marching bands.

like to play one. I just knew that was what I wanted to do when I grew up. From that day on, I begged my father for a flute. He kept telling me that I had to wait until the fourth grade. I kept begging, and he kept saying no. I had a cheap, hollow, aluminum baton I used to twirl. I asked my dad to drill holes in the baton. He did, and we took the rubber ends off it. That was my first flute.

When I finally got a real flute, it changed my life. When I was young, I was painfully shy. I wouldn't raise my hand in class even though I knew the answers. I didn't like to talk out loud. But when I held my flute in my hands, it didn't matter. I could play in front of a million people if I had to. The flute became my voice!

Like Soroka, many young flutists are thrilled when they first get their flute. Yet lots of students who start to learn the flute don't stick with it. Learning the flute is hard. Flute students need to learn to read music. This takes a lot of time and effort. The work means practicing new skills and then putting them all together. It can be quite a while before you're able to play something that sounds good.

**This music teacher helps a young student learning the flute.**

# THAT LOVELY LATIN SOUND

Do you like Latin folk music? If so, the sound of the zampona may appeal to you. The zampona is an early flute. It dates back to the days of the Incas (an ancient people who controlled a large empire in South America by the end of the fifteenth century). The zampona is made of pipes of different lengths. The pipes are bound together in two rows with llama wool or colorful textiles. The zampona is still played in folk music festivals in the Andes Mountains of South America.

These children in the South American country of Bolivia are playing the zampona.

So what makes some flutists go on while others give up? Many longtime flutists believe you have to really love the flute's sound. You also have to have plenty of drive and determination.

Cynthia Kivlan explained how her determination helped her. "I wasn't very good at the flute (when I first started playing)," she said. "The other kids laughed at me because I was out of tune. But that just made me practice even harder. In the end, I became the first-chair flutist (the best flutist in a band or orchestra) in middle school and high school. I just refused to give up."

Are you determined to play the flute? Do you love the way the instrument sounds? Do you look forward to playing it? If so, then the flute is probably right for you.

Learning to play the flute takes a lot of concentration and practice.

# THE SOUND OF WHISTLING WIND

The *quena (right)* is another South American flute that dates back to Incan times. This flute is usually made of bamboo. It has six finger holes and one hole for the thumb. The quena is known for its light, airy sound. Thinking of traveling to the Andes Mountains of South America? If so, you're likely to hear the quena. It's still often played as a solo instrument there.

There's a wonderful legend about the quena. It says that the instrument was invented by a man who wanted to honor the woman he loved. According to the story, the man fell in love with a wealthy Incan princess. But the man was poor, and the princess's father forbade her to marry him. The princess died of a broken heart, and her lover visited her grave every night. While there, he heard the sound of the whistling wind. It reminded him of the princess's lovely voice. So he made a flute that sounded like the wind. It was the quena. Whenever the man heard the quena, he thought of his beloved's beautiful voice.

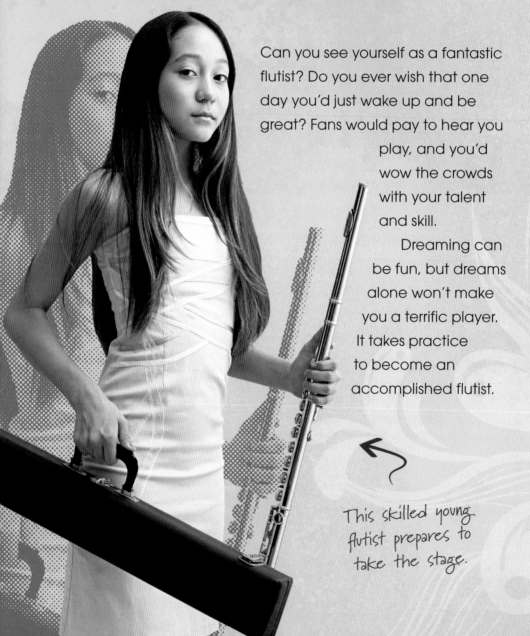

# CHAPTER FOUR

# WHAT DOES IT TAKE TO PLAY THE FLUTE?

Can you see yourself as a fantastic flutist? Do you ever wish that one day you'd just wake up and be great? Fans would pay to hear you play, and you'd wow the crowds with your talent and skill.

Dreaming can be fun, but dreams alone won't make you a terrific player. It takes practice to become an accomplished flutist.

This skilled young flutist prepares to take the stage.

# PRACTICE MAKES PERFECT

How often should you practice? Here's the advice that Carol Naveira-Nicholson has to offer to aspiring flutists.

You've got to practice daily. It's easy to be distracted by things like video games or sports. The fun things you do with friends can make practicing the flute feel like homework. That's why it's important to make your practice time a part of your day. Every day you get up, brush your teeth, and comb your hair. Treat practicing the flute the same way. Set aside a certain time of day as your practice time. At first, you don't need to practice for hours and hours. Even as little as fifteen minutes a day can help. You just have to remember to do it every day.

## BEWARE OF YOUR HAIR!

What does it take to be an excellent flutist? Hard work, dedication...and barrettes? That's right. You may need to buy some hair clips if you want to play the flute. Flutist Leone Buyse explains why: "For a flutist, long, dangling hair can be dangerous. It's got to be pulled away from your face. If it falls into your mouth the sound of the flute will completely disappear."

## NO EXCUSES, PLEASE

If you don't think you're going to practice, you shouldn't commit to playing the flute. If you say you're practicing when you aren't, it will show when you play. Making up excuses won't work either. That can really backfire big time! Here's what happened when flutist Jezabel Joa tried it.

Once when I was in sixth grade, I didn't practice the piece of music I was supposed to learn. The teacher saw that I couldn't play it and looked very annoyed. I didn't want to tell her that I hadn't practiced. Instead, I decided to tell her that I couldn't see the notes on the sheet music. That would only lead to worse things, but I didn't know that then. The teacher later called my mother and told her what happened. My mother became concerned. She made an appointment for me to see the eye doctor. By then I was too embarrassed to tell anyone the truth. So I just went along with it.

I wasn't able to fool the eye doctor. He told my mother that there was nothing wrong with my eyesight. That's when the truth came out. I had to admit that I'd lied. I felt horrible. I wished I had just put in the practice time. It would have been so much easier for everyone.

## A PRACTICE PLAN

Some music teachers want their students to have a practice plan to help keep their practicing on track. When you set a practice plan, you define your goals. That should help you get to where you want to go musically.

Part of your plan should be about how many minutes you spend practicing every day. There's no hard-and-fast rule. Different teachers may suggest different amounts of practice time. And the practice time required may vary from student to student. "Every person is different," flutist Wendy Willis explained. "Music may come naturally to some and not so naturally to others. What one person might achieve in minutes, may take hours for another."

Figuring out the finger work is essential to playing the flute.

# A PRACTICE TIP
# THAT REALLY WORKS

Want a surefire way to improve your playing skills? Wendy Willis offered this tip. "To be a good musician takes many hours of practice on your instrument. You sometimes have to play the same passage over and over and over. My music teacher always told me, 'Keep playing it until you can do it correctly five times.' So if I was on time number four and made a mistake...ugh! I'd wipe the slate clean and start over with number one."

So how much daily practice should you plan for? See what works best for you. Discuss it with your teacher. Between the two of you, you should be able to come up with an amount of time that suits you.

Being focused should also be part of your practice plan. When you practice, you shouldn't be thinking about a TV show you watched last night or the party you're going to this weekend. Practice your flute the same way an athlete trains for a competition. Work hard at it, and think about which skills you'd like to improve. Kat Epple offered this tip to young flutists: "Never play through a song just to play it correctly. Play it better, and try to improve your performance each time you play it."

# SURVIVING ONSTAGE

Even if you stick to your practice plan and always try your best, things can still go wrong when it's time to perform. You can have a memory slip. You can accidentally miss a note. Outdoor performances can be particularly problematic. Rain can spoil an outdoor concert. Sheet music has blown off stands. Here's what happened to flutist Terri Mitchell during an outdoor performance. "I took a deep breath before I started to play," she recalled. "To my shock, I inhaled an insect. I choked and couldn't play. There were tears coming out of my eyes. The violinist and violist were laughing so hard that they couldn't play either."

Being prepared for a performance is an important part of becoming an expert flutist.

# DOING A BIT TOO MUCH!

Flutist Nina Perlove explained a funny experience she had while performing onstage in junior high school. "I had a theater performance and an orchestra concert on the same night. I couldn't miss either performance. So I had to play my orchestra concert wearing the costume from my play. The audience was staring at me because everyone else in the orchestra was wearing all black. I, however, was in an orange dress with a long wig. It all turned out okay, but now, I am always careful to check my calendar before I schedule any concerts. I want to make sure I don't have to be in two places at the same time!"

Things are bound to go wrong at times. The trick is in how you handle it. Try not to let it throw you. Always do your best to keep on playing. The saying, "Don't let them see you sweat," applies here. Kat Epple put it this way. "You will play a wrong note in a performance. This is something that happens to every musician. It even happens to the best ones. Just keep on playing. Don't get flustered. Remember that the people listening to you really want you to do well. Take a quick deep breath and just keep going. Don't be embarrassed. Be proud, and remember it is a great accomplishment to play music."

## THE MAGIC OF THE MUSIC

Whether or not you have a perfect performance, keep your focus on the music. That's all that really matters in the end. If you give your all to your flute and to your music, you'll feel good knowing that you've done your very best. And you'll be able to share the magic of beautiful flute music with those around you. For many people, there's nothing better.

The best way to become an accomplished flutist is to practice.

# QUIZ: IS THE FLUTE RIGHT FOR YOU?

*Which of these statements describes you best? Please record your answers on a separate sheet of paper.*

**1. If at first you don't succeed,**

   **A.** You try, try again. You like to finish what you start. People say you're the determined type.

   **B.** You feel that a lack of success means it wasn't meant to be. You prefer to try something else you may be better at.

**2. When you hear a good piece of music,**

   **A.** You get really into all the sounds. You feel as if you could listen to the piece forever!

   **B.** You think it sounds good, but you don't usually get too absorbed in it. You'd rather spend time working on art or learning new soccer moves than listening closely to music.

**3. When you're doing a task that requires fine motor skills,**

   **A.** Your fingers are quick and nimble. Detailed tasks are fun for you.

   **B.** You tend to drop things or get frustrated. Taking bike rides or playing video games is more up your alley than working with your hands.

**4. When you picture yourself playing an instrument in your school band,**

   **A.** You imagine yourself playing something small. You think petite can be neat! The tuba is not for you.

   **B.** You imagine yourself playing the bass drum, the cello . . . anything big! You love the sound and feel of a large musical instrument.

**5. When you think about practicing your instrument,**

   **A.** You get really excited. You think studying an instrument sounds like fun!

   **B.** You like music, but you can think of other things you'd rather do. Giving up free time to practice every day doesn't sound worth it.

**Were your answers mostly A's?**

**If so, the flute may just be the right choice for you!**

# GLOSSARY

**body joint:** the longest part of the flute. Both the head joint and the foot joint connect to it. Most of the flute's keys are on the body joint.

**ensemble:** a small musical group

**foot joint:** a part of the flute that has a few keys and tone holes

**head joint:** the part of the flute that is held closest to your mouth

**improvisation:** making up parts of the music you play while you are playing it

**jazz:** a form of music characterized by loose structure and improvisation

**key:** the part of the flute that a flutist presses down on to play notes

**lip plate:** the place where your lower lip rests when you play the flute. The lip plate is also known as the embouchure plate.

**mouth hole:** a small opening on the flute's lip plate. A flute player blows air over the mouth hole to produce a sound.

**pitch:** the highness or lowness of a sound

**solo:** a musical performance in which a performer plays alone

**woodwind family:** a group of instruments that produce sound when air is blown over or through them

# SOURCE NOTES

7   Kat Epple, e-mail message to author, August 4, 2009.

19   Carol Naveira-Nicholson, interview with author, July 17, 2009.

20–21   Cynthia Kivlan, e-mail message to author, September 1, 2009.

22–24   Christine Soroka, e-mail message to author, July 22, 2009.

26   Kivlan.

29   Naveira-Nicholson.

29   Leone Buyse, e-mail message to author, May 31, 2009.

30   Jezabel Joa, telephone conversation with author, July 23, 2009.

31   Wendy Willis, e-mail message to author, July 21, 2009.

32  Willis.

32  Epple.

33  Terri Mitchell, e-mail message to author, August 6, 2009.

34  Nina Perlove, e-mail message to author, May 29, 2009.

34–35  Epple.

## SELECTED BIBLIOGRAPHY

Baines, Anthony. *Woodwind Instruments and Their History.* New York: Dover Publications, 1994.

Harrison, Howard. *How to Play the Flute: Everything You Need to Know to Play the Flute.* Gordonville, VA: St. Martin's Griffin, 2002.

Powell, Ardal. *The Flute.* Cumberland, RI: Yale University Press, 2003.

Toff, Nancy. *The Flute Book: A Complete Guide for Students and Performers.* Cary, NC: Oxford University Press, 1996.

## FOR MORE INFORMATION

Dallas Symphony Orchestra: Kids
http://www.dsokids.com
Visit this website to learn about the flute and listen to the sounds it makes. Don't miss the link to fun music-related games!

Enchanted Learning: Musical Instruments
http://www.enchantedlearning.com/music/instruments
Check out this site for information, printouts, and activities related to musical instruments.

Figley, Marty Rhodes. *John Greenwood's Journey to Bunker Hill.* Minneapolis: Millbrook Press, 2011. This book tells the story of fifteen-year-old fife player John Greenwood, who enlists to fight and play his fife in the American Revolution. A 10-page Reader's Theater script is included with the story.

Josephson, Judith Pinkerton. *Bold Composer: A Story about Ludwig van Beethoven.* Minneapolis: Millbrook Press, 2007. Josephson tells the engaging life story of Beethoven, one of the world's best-loved composers.

Kenney, Karen Latchana. *Cool Rock Music: Create and Appreciate What Makes Music Great!* Edina, MN: Abdo, 2008. This book introduces rock music and the instruments used to play it.

# THE FLUTISTS WHO HELPED WITH THIS BOOK

This book could not have been written without the help of these flutists. All provided great insights into what it is like to love and play the flute.

### LEONE BUYSE
Leone Buyse was formerly principal flutist of the Boston Symphony and Boston Pops orchestras. She is a professor at Rice University's Shepherd School of Music.

### KAT EPPLE
Kat Epple is an Emmy-Award-winning and Grammy-nominated composer and flutist. She has composed music for television and film scores and performed for audiences in numerous countries.

### JEZABEL JOA
Jezabel Joa is a professional flutist with the Miami Lyric Opera.

### CYNTHIA KIVLAN
Cynthia Kivlan is a professional flutist from Miami, Florida, who attended the University of Miami Frost School of Music. She performs throughout South Florida with various ensembles and as a soloist.

### TERRI MITCHELL
Terri Mitchell is the principle flutist with the Ars Flores Symphony Orchestra. She also teaches flute at the University of Miami and conducts the Flute Choir there.

### CAROL NAVEIRA-NICHOLSON
Carol Naveira-Nicholson is the principal flutist with the Miami Symphony Orchestra.

### NINA PERLOVE
Nina Perlove has a doctorate degree in musical arts and has won numerous awards for her flute music. She is regarded as one of the most listened-to classical flutists of her generation.

### CHRISTINE SOROKA
Christine Soroka is a professional flutist and the owner of Pittsburgh Music Live.

### WENDY WILLIS
Wendy Willis has played the flute with numerous orchestras throughout Michigan, Indiana, and Florida including the Naples Philharmonic and the Southwest Florida Symphony.

# INDEX

# PHOTO ACKNOWLEDGMENTS

The images in this book are used with the permission of: © Yang Jay/Dreamstime.com, p. 1; © Stockbyte/Getty Images, p. 3; © Comstock Images/Getty Images, pp. 4-5; © Stefan M. Prager/Redferns/Getty Images, p. 5; © Ariel Skelley/CORBIS, p. 6; © Vincent Giordano/Dreamstime.com, pp. 8-9; © RubberBall/Alamy, p. 10; © Patti Ouderkirk/WireImage/Getty Images, p. 11; © Tim Mosenfelder/Getty Images, p. 12; © Andrew Lepley/Redferns/Getty Images, p. 13; © JMEnternational/Redferns/Getty Images, p. 14; © Elena Milevska/Dreamstime.com, p. 15; © Jim Cummins/Taxi/Getty Images, p. 16; © Barros & Barros/Photographer's Choice/Getty Images, p. 17; © Ingram Publishing/Photolibrary, p. 18; © Kuttig-People/Alamy, p. 19; © Flying Colours Ltd/Digital Vision/Getty Images, p. 20; © Jstudio/Dreamstime.com, p. 21; © Jeff Greenberg/Alamy, p. 22; © Jim West/Alamy, p. 23; © Elyse Lewin/Photographer's Choice/Getty Images, p. 24; © Aizar Raldes/AFP/Getty Images, p. 25; © Adie Bush/Cultura/Getty Images, p. 26; © iStockphoto.com/Kristian Peetz, p. 27; © Image Source/Getty Images, p. 28; © Shargaljut/Dreamstime.com, p. 31; © David L. Moore/Alamy, p. 33; © Matthias Hauser/imagebroker.net/Photolibrary, p. 35.

Cover: © Yang Jay/Dreamstime.com (top and bottom); © Vincent Giordano/Dreamstime.com (middle).